Black Like That

Black Like That

Poems from a Conduit

Ray Jane

Ray Jane Productions LLC

Copyright © 2023 by Ray Jane
New York, NY

Cover Art by **Oladimeji Alaka**

All rights reserved. No part of this book may be reproduced in any manner whatsoever without written permission from Ray Jane except in the case of brief quotations embodied in critical articles and reviews. Addresses, questions, comments, send to: ItsRayJane@gmail.com

Visit my website: ItsRayJane.com

FIRST EDITION
ISBN: 978-1-73793-640-4
Available as an electronic book: ISBN 978-1-73793-641-1
Available as downloadable audio file: ISBN 978-1-7379364-2-8

Printed in the United States of America

CONTENTS

DEDICATION ix

Milepost 1 1

What Music Do Your Bones Hold? 3

Right Before the Lights Come On 4

Unsung Stanzas of the Star Spangled Banner 5

The Drums 6

Milepost 2 8

The Game of Life 10

Medicine Woman 11

Every Wicked Thing I Need To Survive 12

Universe of She 13

Bag Lady 15

Milepost 3 16

CONTENTS

Dealer 18

Primordial Pantoum 22

A Bop for Ketanji 23

No One Asked Us 24

Milepost 4 25

Thirteen 27

What to Do When the Fruit Ain't Strange 28

July 4th: America Might Be a Ho 30

Peeped My Power at the Zoo 34

Milepost 5 36

Human Jigsaw 37

AAS 231 39

Black Thigh Thaumaturgy 41

Black Econ 42

Milepost 6 44

Possession 46

For the Black Body 48

CONTENTS

For Sandra   51

Daunte Wright   53

‖ Milepost 7   54

Blacker   56

Mutiny   57

Cutlass   59

Pump Action   62

‖ Milepost 8   67

He Was in His Alt-Right Mind   69

Politikin'   71

Georgia's On My Mind   75

Privilege   78

American Dream-Robbed   80

‖ Milepost 9   82

Name– the first displacement   84

Unknown   85

Churning   87

CONTENTS

I-dentities 89

Milepost 10 90

Sharecropper's Grands 92

Cotton 93

Long Blood 95

Healing in Fields of Yarrow 97

Moratorium 99

Screaming 100

Milepost 11 102

Ain't I a Woman? 104

Brown 105

Four Women Flying 107

HOLLA 108

Black Love 112

My Black Is 117

ACKNOWLEDGEMENTS 121
REVIEWS 123
ABOUT THE AUTHOR 126

I dedicate this book of poems– this offering from an observant, but still learning creature– to the melanated. To my Black family for shielding me and showing me what I need to survive and to thrive. To my Black family that raised me to crave the fire of scotch bonnet peppers, the truth in who killed Cornbread, and the knowledge that I am God's. May these words pay homage to how you persist in a world constructed to undervalue all things associated with the presence of color, free-thinking intellect, and our right to be all things including Black AND delicate.

Milepost 1

The First Thing the Dead Might Say

"Who your people?"

What Music Do Your Bones Hold?

After Mayda Del Valle

These bones vibrate
slapping a line of white ivories on card table
they shake, lovers of booming bass
bellowing forever like the shape of 808
like, the dope boys rolling slow down the block
rhythms heating concrete provide music sheets

you can hear these bones coming
rumbling hood symphonies
old heads become slowly bopping gray domes
offering quick glimpses of respect
recognizing similar cadence in my joints

twisting in and out of 4-4 tempos
the realness rising up out my drop top
over windows rolled down by hand
earning it's breeze

it be, funkdafied, fried, died, and blow-dried
but still, rocking freshly crisped curlers
in the melodies of hair salon spilling tea behind me

It's summertime and it's
summertimeeeee & the music is eaaaasyyyyy
Immortal symphonies
aging gracefully in my marrow

Right Before the Lights Come On

This dance is proof that all rhythms really love me
Unaware why divine overfilled cup
rotund hind-quarters splitting mixes up
dividing decibels is light work dear
This rear, rides beat, front row, passenger seat
complete revolutions encircle me
You can't out-twerk me, whole spine built from jelly
Don't mind belly baby, hot sauce in my feet
No night complete, sweat dripping, shirt clinging
shaking, bell ranging, discarded partner
don't do-si-doh, this magic four-four beat
ain't no one, two, three; boom cat symphony
String section middle screams, horns reviving
serpentine, thriving, couplets forgetting
crowded winin' ting bashment champion
Dancehall queen, gathering admiration
salacious eyes undress taste beaded sweat
lights up, quickly forget, dark disguises regret

* After Twerk Villanelle by Porsha Olayiwola

Unsung Stanzas of the Star Spangled Banner

The trick is
these spangles start to look
a lot like hanging questions
In these same ol' colonies
we circle back to wack like
nooses, oops it's
a slight of tongue

This freedom song, this freedom, this free
Dumb expensive
The stripes we paint on backs,
our art graphic, raised, undeniable,
Horrible, Splendid.

Penny for your dreams!
O' tis of thee'll spend it, then

Send you a bill for your culture
Til' you crow

Go ahead and sing chile!
Ain't nothin' left but music and your foes

Gleaming in this twilight
Giving proof, in hindsight, of night
that your Black is still there
Where oh where can a nigga shed fear?!

When blue rockets red glare
When our freedom stay bursting in air.

The Drums

the drums recall my language

speak fluently to my people
pounding pathways for the dead to rise
a spell that always binds

the drums

my people are reborn   over
stretched hides
our lives persistent   percussion
our impacts require   vibration
somehow
       remembering
           the way
             back
knocking, my body
unlocking at its joints
eyelids close, sacrificing sight
to properly ground

all feeling from here
arms lifting from here
shoulders catching old rhythms
rolling themselves into tides
too-late buoy, retrieving the lost
lifting brined beauty

the drummed beat shifts
involuntarily my body dips
my soul slips, a bit

BLACK LIKE THAT

out of this vessel
aware and also *between*
I know this urn
is now a shared thing, I become
an ancient record skipping

hips join heartbeat
drums become electricity

shoes are removed from feet, connection
requiring foundations return to the earth
communicating magics make movements
mimic auras—
oscillating between indigo, and violet
at times, rotations are violent

I
surrender permission to whoever inside this,
needed to worship,
be un-bottled from this carbonated existence
all in perimeter witness, feel something recognizing free

the drums
making me mirror,
reflecting memories that are not mine

the drums
reminding all within reach,
that your body,
still knows your language.

Milepost 2

Grain Memory

"Always follow your first mind"

The Game of Life

* After "We Should Make a Documentary about Spades" by Terrance Hayes

In momma's house
we don't play no games
Even when Game
is on the table

Every card drawn is battle
We become swordsmen at dinner

Learning early why daddy
made momma his bookkeeper

Grits were mixed with lessons
Daddy stored cards under foot
so we walked with stealth
expecting to be cheated

Slaps of ivory tore through ears
So we learned
how to celebrate
To take up space
To feel victory vibrate our bones

At penultimate,
the kitchen table reminded us
that going bubble was possible

Medicine Woman

Medicine woman pulling my card
threw my bones in a circle
tabulated,
I waited

Threw the salty residue of centuries of bloated
dreams drowned. Tabulated,
had to throw the whole ocean in
I waited

Threw in both strands of my DNA
tried to bargain the trauma bit out
she refused, went on tabulating,
I waited

Threw three small bags of sand onto my scales,
raised a hand, stopped my protest– a dowry
for my religion due. She said this was only
a sampling, went on tabulating,
I waited

Before she threw the last weight, she gently
slid silk gloves over her skin, I expected white, the care
she took showed up as green, gentle, with the speed
respect necessitates. A single feather was placed.
We held our breath. Spirit went on, tabulating,
We waited

Every Wicked Thing I Need To Survive

* After Elegies by Roberto Carlos Garcia

The bottom of my favorite pot is Black
with residues of old mes I cooked off the bone
its got the sweet of me commingling effortlessly
with my current curries, I got gumbo
for that too honey, get you a bowl
I'm makin' biscuits for all the love
I'm serving up. I got all the ingredients
in my pot

Universe of She

I was born out of melody, tapping feet when reciting
to breadcrumb myself
Between dimensions I return to me riding rhythms
Miles and Coltrane combine to explode me back into this timeline

I arrive, covered in my grandmother's rubies, abundance
Finally finding me in a past life, made present

There we are, rings of gold erecting neck
Unbending in my intention, eyes Black like the coal
in my 8th momma's steely spirit,

I resurrect royalty remembering myself
Translate my infinity into mathematical equations, lemniscate
the likes of which the great pyramids use to communicate with

Every 4000 years, I learn to realign between clef notes

Correspond with my past lives in tongue of the Pleiades
Kiss my green skinned husband, forgive him for letting me travel
portals alone,

I am what I have always been, singular
Enough, too tough to be timed,
stretching galaxies in my brass arms,

I hold the world up, inspect its worthiness of my return
find it lacking, cut off 7 locs to gift to my future selves
Tell them to plant me in *every* wonder, give us something to do
on the next go 'round.

RAY JANE

I marvel at how many universes
I got doorknocker earrings on in,
tuck my bejeweled crown under fitted
in at least 10 dimensions, bop my way back to real rap

Spit a hot 16 on my way back to Mars, among the stars

I remain an original, great mother Spirit, Sankofa with my seeds
I rode a saxophone's sexy neck back
to impregnate me and my own mind
with symphonies of reasons never to settle,

I open gold-dusted lips
scream joy into the darkness that embodies everything
honor this forever warrior spirit, kicking up dust JUST
to escape the catchers

Bag Lady

Broke my own jaw,
so my grand momma
could finally get out
I unhinged her with a loud
C   R   A   C   K!
Before I knew it, we were singing

I'm finna miss my bus!
Curse this new need to speak, its
Got me missing connections, cuz I
Forget too quickly, the freedom in
Speech costs listening. I'm
Holding on to how it felt when ignored
Yelling again, for all the reasons, no longer
Fearing being loud and wrong

Got to put these bags down
Emptied me of need to be
Perfect. Threw my back out trying out no
Boundaries, fell flat on my face when
Listening seemed less sexy than my own
Voice, doubting me damn near cost me
All of me, but damn if believing
Ain't the biggest bill yet

Milepost 3

Inquiry

INQUIRY

DEAR EDITOR—Please allow me to make inquiry for my mother, Nancy Love. We were separated about the year 1850, in Mississippi. I was then but an infant of about 9 months. We belonged to Anderson Moss. He sold my mother to Mr. Ned Herndon, a speculator in slaves. He sold her to Mrs. Hooker, a widow in Jackson, Miss. It was then that I heard from her last—about the year 1853. My mother wrote to Miss Love Mass as to her whereabouts. Any information relative to her will be very thankfully received. Address me at Maysfield, Milam county, Texas.

LUCY CLARKE.

Southwestern Christian Advocate (New Orleans, LA), March 18, 1880

"Lucy Clarke searching for her mother Nancy Love," Southwestern Christian Advocate (New Orleans, LA), March 18, 1880, Last Seen: Finding Family After Slavery, accessed May 3, 2023, https://informationwanted.org/items/show/1457

Dealer

As a Black woman
I BEEN dealin'
Since I made the deck
and I ain't stopped yet

Even with my cards
out of my hands
since my Kings were stolen
from our lands
Skipping, missing lessons
tryna' raise this full house
on sinking sand

Sometimes,
wheelin', to make the ends meet

I'll, flush these Jokers

I'll, declare war

I'll, call *Bullshit!*

Don't let me get a lil' rum
or a lil' gin
Don't, let me start
playing to win
Start, pullin' my blades
if you book any of my spades
I'll draw, for mines

Get perverse and reverse

BLACK LIKE THAT

on an occupier, black yo' eye jack,
with my mind, I'll run up in yo' mine

Bust you with these pinochles

I, Queen
bend my body, like bridge
beg my people
to walk swiftly, over it
to return, to Ourselves

I BEEN strong
I BEEN capable
I BEEN runnin' game
since Egyptian rat screw

Stretching across infinity
my eights crazy, this poker face
saves me, in mixed company

They think they jailing me
but I BEEN
camping, in your concentration
eyes wide, tracking constellations
Harriet-ing all my nations

With, bleeding hands
I, teach my babies this
Immortal Technique

Bait, then hide their hooks
then let them go fish
teach them to seek
their own, version of rich

She raisin' you
Gold-dipped alchemists
wielding so much magic
they make white baloney
into a dish

RAY JANE

They all bet on this
place your bid on her Whist
she, on everybody's wish-list

Let them babies stand on my pride
tell them every place they be
is the wild

But, in Texas, I hold 'em
extra close, hustle,
'cuz I gotta keep their necks
free from rope
keep it slack, then stack,
flip, and spread our tarot

But, damn
this old maid is gettin' tired
playing, cuz she know
she can't fold
but fearing
loss of mo jo

Sometimes, it's a NO-go
Sometimes, this back breaks up under the load
Sometimes, I don't want to care
Sometimes, I want to be solitaire

At times, she feel nil
but even then, she stay trill

Even when, ain't no water
in her well

'Cuz the whole world drinks,
so much so
that the whole world thinks

You can-asta
sista to do more

Ask her

BLACK LIKE THAT

to hold you up, ike she ain't BEEN
the floor

Prints on her back, like the lash,
she cut that deck fast,
hoping for the right suit

Praying it ain't too late
to win back the loot
But she an old tree,
she the first root

So, she keeps it close to chest
store her water, get her rest

Then,
show her hand when she
manifest

Then,
sweep up these ends
and make the best
of whatever is left

Primordial Pantoum

Primordial, my goop been telling the same story—
tale of obsidian bodies   over-mined
natural springs demolished or   damned and
realms where that narrative is preposterous

Tale of obsidian bodies   over-mined
remains a 3-dimensional storyline
realms where that narrative is preposterous
running parallel to this reality, but not, close enough

Remains, a 3-dimensional storyline
so the physics needed to surmount otherness, is still redacted
running parallel to this reality, but not, close enough
my freedom probably still whispered in alien cockpits

So, the physics needed to surmount otherness, still redacted
but the truth inked in my DNA calls me hybrid
my freedom probably still whispered in alien cockpits
Primordial, my goop been telling the same story

A Bop for Ketanji

A Black woman attempted to ascend, damn near
forbidden on this stolen land. We   bit Our fingertips
watched her climb, peace, an uncanny perspiration, softening
the anguish carried in a Black woman's cheeks, collected
She double-dutched questions looped like
noose, but you can't hang   what you can't   confuse

Ketanji been had it

overqualified, and vying for a seat beneath her
a Black woman waits
credentials so tall, the asses began to assume foolish posture
presented new math, miscalculated in baseless insinuations
presiding over pedophiles somehow led to summation-- imposter
for Her/Us   quiet   is the only form of proper   allowed
a Black woman's rage must not be seen, at least   not   aloud, so
safely, behind tv screens We screamed, the shame of Our America
again, public   again, obscene   the way a Black phoenix has to die
before resurrecting

Ketanji been   had it

Never behind, but the finish line kept moving, finally the allies
began to practice what they preached, then
a Brother spoke strength to truth, told the whole world that She,
that We, were worthy, so necessary a tear dropped brazenly,
never before had I seen   a Black woman sort her flowers
above the dirt   and then be named a name worth repeating
Supreme

Ketanji   been had it

No One Asked Us

* After Nikki Giovanni "But Since You finally asked (A Poem commemorating the 10th Anniversary of the Slave Memorial at Mount Vernon)"

Some white man along the way decided I should be at war with my dimensions. I ain't just talkin' hips– what made all my mommas magic mitochondrial. I mean, *all* my parts, at odds.

This Blackness became an open invitation for redefining, as if I couldn't recognize myself without a Blue eye's perspective. So from someone else's vantage I appeared angry, when smiling; like I'm stealing, when shopping, cash in hand.

Somewhere along the way, I became uncannily ugly. Like they don't see me sittin' here in my Sunday's best. Perhaps, I'm wearing the wrong religion again.

Milepost 4

Who is the human?

"Where they do that at?"

Thirteen

Thirteen!

Colonies, colonized me
Hung me from every tree

Thirteen!

Amendments amending me
With moniker of beast

Thirteen!

Reasons to continue slavery,
unreasonable, to grab for free,
treat me like I'm only 3/5ths complete

Thirteen!

Stripes on flag, naked ropes noosin'
Seems seams are ripping
Winds of change whipping
White so red, but American been crippin'

Thirteen!

So mean, so mean, got elevators jumpin'
From twelve to fifteen, most salient curse
I've seen, while alive, but then,
There was forty-five.

What to Do When the Fruit Ain't Strange

*For Donte Perez Jones

ANOTHER Black man HUNG, 2 days before Juneteenth
another STRANGE FRUIT swung, HEARD THE ANCESTORS
MOAN
so he would not be   ALONE   in the trees   in the night
far from family, DYING ALONE IN THE DARK
DYING ALONE because we DARE BE ALIVE
dying alone, again

NO SURPRISE   still   wets my eyes
AGAIN, and it's no surprise
AGAIN   REFUSING TO BE NUMB   to my own demise
HE is I   SHE is I   if YOU DIE, I DIE   EVERY time
old PROMISEs made TO THIS skin
hissed truths still NOT WRITTEN in the CONSTITUTION
NO LAW TO OUTLAW HOW I STILL   swing
how   MY BODY   is STILL   STRANGE

As I clamor for joy,
as I CELEBRATE   THE "BREAKING" of old chains
CAN'T convince my spirit
REST in peace, we   STILL DISTRACTED   BY the SCENT
MY FAMILIAR DEATH,   WET BLOOD   in my nares
MY ROTTING FREEDOM   AINT   NO THEORY!
BUT YET we step   LEAP OVER it   MY RACE
in CRITICAL condition, STILL FOUND
SWINGING

DEATH IN OUR AIR

BLACK LIKE THAT

they KEEP death in MY FEARS
while squeezing LIFE out of our lungs
while THEIR   QUIET COUSINS   look on
WHISPER sentiments of TOGETHERNESS,
while THEIR   uncles, BROTHERS,   EVEN   their MOTHERS
swing us,   kill us,   HAVE US
dying ALONE, in the dark

LAST NERVE SEVERED, reacting
handholding with GOD   to handle this dharma
psychological trauma GOT ME IRATE,
survival got us TOO SEDATE
again   WE WAIT on the   KARMA
HESITATION in my TRIGGER fingers
do I share it, do I post it, DO I DARE?
UNSTRING ANOTHER, we been unreeling
feels like an unreal thing!
FIGHTing this UNFEELING!
GOT TO KEEP FEELING! HOW CAN I STOP FEELING?!!!
SUCH DEATH should ALWAYS FEEEEEEEL like
RAGEEEEEEEE! RAGEEEEEE! RAGEEEEE!
GOT TO TELL MY STORY   BEFORE   THEY BURN
THE PAGE!

SILENCE killed my people
SILENCE is KKKilling   MY   PEOPLE!
SILENCE, not rope!
SILENCE, NOT your incessant apologies!
SILENCE, IS A GUN!
SILENCE, HAS NOT RUN OUT OF AMMUNITION, yet!

2 DAYS before JUNETEENTH
the only gift we get
ANOTHER BODY HUNG
LET ANOTHER BODY SWING
IN THESE TREES   HATE   DON'T   CHANGE!
THE FRUIT AINT STRANGE!
JUST ANOTHER   DYING   BLACK
                                BODY
                                        ALONE!
AGAIN!   and   I   FEEL!

July 4th: America Might Be a Ho

America got the fattest ass
the way she just showing it all the time
She crass– Got that thing just hangin' out
Make you want to smack that, no shame
Mad nasty

According to its own standards
America might be a ho
She stuntin', a slut, a fast woman
Bussin' it for everybody to see
Ass up, head down
shame crown

Poppin' it for whoever got them
Dollas. With its people as the pole
America keeps that ass swole, working
them souls, She cajoles

My brother tried to say it's pancake
Nah it's the juiciest, so juicy
It's still in bidnez, nocturnal and barely hidden

Acrobattin' 'til daylight, then walkin' out the night
Like, nothin' happened

But yo
Let me not diminish real hardworkin' hos

America lazy
She got mad moves, but she a old pole worker
Blockin' at the polls, Sis been spinnin' since

| 30 |

BLACK LIKE THAT

Reconstruction, even before then, She was straddlin'
natives, renaming them Indians. Her
first stage name Buffalo Betty, but had to change it
For political correctness

First to shake weight, bury history and fake the wake
Get up on the casket and serve the mourning cake
Seductively licking frosted amber waves of grain
Let me say it again
That ass done twisted cries into sangin'
That thang been thangin', Got security gang bangin'
Lettin' all her homies hit it

Confidently, She admit it
By her own standards America a ho
So, on her b-day
Expect her to throw it, forget all the hearts broken
She keeps her death pussy wet, keeps
churning, hips, turning slave ships to cells,
6x6—

The first trick, if you think she ain't yo pimp
you a silly simp, cuz while you throw your dollas
and eat your own wings
you don't feel your own cheeks clappin'
to her music

Hypnotic— Red, white, and blue
making wickedness erotic, morals chaotic
But shake that ass!

Get that money honey, It's all game til'
it ain't funny, 'til' that ass got you runnin'
Wondering how you got into stilettos
Where your coverings went, why
You star dusted on stage, America got you bent
Tried to teach you how to shake, but you too late
Too soft, can't move in the key of hate.

But hey, soon you'll catch the rhythm,
it's the American way

RAY JANE

And   on   July   4th
You can Sambo yo ass off
On that b-day setlist now
the injections finally got you soft
Sooo Cannn Youuu Seeeeeee
why fire works?
Light up the world, and call it a twerk

America got you tweekin', she leakin'
And you soakin' wet, dying just
to be up under her dress. Say less!
She shake her ass while she confess
to caging dreamers babies
She considered that finesse
Sacrilegious and scantily dressed
AMERICAN ass does it best

WoRLd CHamPIon Droppppp!

She'll send you to the Olympics
then reject ya' magic, if you dare try
to headline, She dig and find
any reason to keep that lime
Keep that light off ya mind
Dig and find, She dig, and fine
Sell you premium roll and call cops
Every time

Lower bar when you flip outside ya britches
Change the scorecard to keep her riches
She de-throne any fish tryna swim in her sea
With they own natural on

Cut ya mic, and turn her jam back on
Go shorty!
It's ya birthday!
Ocean on fire on your earth day!

Seems apropos, still
bring the sparklers though!

BLACK LIKE THAT

cuz America stay lit, no matter how it go

She gon' shake that ass,
While we throwin and drown in her remix
Steppin', steppin' good, we stay steppin' in it

While she wild and not so discreetly disastrous
Yellin' *"Girl! Turn that destruction up*
Thas my shit!"

But why ain't you dancin'
Ain't you independent?

Peeped My Power at the Zoo

Peeped my power in an enclosure. Trappers passing, admiring the wildness of me. Couldn't take my eyes off her either. She lay so calmly in the fluffy green fakeness, I couldn't tell if the zoo had her, or if she *let them* keep her.

A shy colonizer could barely stare too long— my power's salacious stretching in direct sunlight was, obviously, not for everyone. Yet closer, a different invader, standing upright, as if willing herself higher, nearer to her cage than most would dare, seemed to need to be imposing near my power. I rolled my eyes, unable to decide what was worse: the cringeworthy display of how hate can shrink, or Philip Levine over there pontificating about what they must feed my power. Stepped a few feet away from him, while She, my power, went on soaking up herself. I enjoyed the slow chuckle that escaped me.

As if she heard me, familiar frequency in our humor, my power locked eyes with me. We shared consciousness– her third eye, slanted by nature, mine, drawn on. This made me laugh harder, she was funnier in a shared perspective. I enjoyed her quick snide thoughts , naming her challenging admirers, seeming to respect their gall. Appalled, I asked her with unblinking eyes if she was happy, enclosed. Feeling no need to answer, she sent me grace instead. Somehow, I knew I was asking the wrong question...to the wrong me.

Naively, I went on asking questions, as if I did not know her. Instinctively, she yawned, when asked about her lineage. Appearing careless, she mentioned that she has always been in the family. Telling stories of her glory days, when she was allowed to roam free. She became withdrawn when recounting an instance of overindulgence— I understood that there were casualties.

Not realizing the diminishing distance to understanding, I glided near her, caught glimpse of myself in her vanity. Outraged! I snapped into reality, demanding to speak to the owner. Needing to comprehend who could toy with a creature's freedom like this. On-lookers peered at me quizzically, none motivated, some shielding their kids. She yawned again. Security eventually ambled over, also, confused, saying wild things

BLACK LIKE THAT

like *are you ok?* Or *do you need to sit down?* In full *I NEED TO SEE THE MANAGER*
I went on demanding explanations, never expecting the world to tilt. She yawned.

Security brought me to the large sign, hanging, apparently, right above my power's
enclosure. My family name in lights, inviting people to view her. Incensed, in only the
way embarrassment could provoke, self-righteousness bolstering my ire, I snatched the
master keys, bum-rushed security, and hopped in my ever-ready crusade cart. Feeling
wild myself, decided my first act as noblewoman would be to release my power.
Rounding my bends, on two-wheels- avoiding hastiness, a separate lesson, for a differ-
ent poem- Adrenaline drowning out the sounds of descendents of the trans-atlantic
market all around, finally getting the intimacy they've craved. All of us knowing, if my
wild truth gets free, eager to greet their voyeurism with toothy reality.

Heart slamming in my ears, soon became dull. I found her cage door swung ajar.
Initially, enraged– Having missed my own savior moment. I smirk instead. Still,
respecting her humor.

| 35 |

Milepost 5

"Chopped Up Niggers"

− a puzzle game created by the McLoughlin
Brothers, 1874

Human Jigsaw

Consider the absurdity in sectioning a Black body
Hacksaws taken to our humanity daily
Ogling public eying the lusciousness in our swing
Powerless spirits pull our physicality to pieces
Partition parents to penitentiaries- planned parenthood
Eager to keep cap on our blooms, cage our gardens
Deforestation also happens in neighborhoods

Unrooted oaks booked for loitering, as if
Penal institutions didn't unearth them first

Nah, something smells like the pungence of planning
Impossible to ignore, spirit hounding the scent
Going after it, familiar rabidness, ravaging
Going back to old days, old ways of capturing
Earth-bound spirits, laying traps, still
Rounding us up, hushing guts with delicious
Semi-satisfying carcinogens, dulling our signaling

Plans popping up all over, conspiracies of
Un-aliving we, now unredacted, public
Zion emerging from our unmuffled stories
Zeale of ancestry climbing out of silence
Lakes like Lanier so crowded now killing on contact
Easier to feed secret/sleeping beast immediately
Submerge the truth beside Black bodies

Too many pieces realigning
Ornate flesh emerging from false narratives

RAY JANE

Princes made inmates, numbers
Unnamed, stripped again
Too familiar to be willingly digested, again

Thrones begin to regurgitate bad minds
Obelisks raise, rename themselves tekhenu
Gross memory of reason for structure, recovering
Each corner of Black consciousness
Trying out our telepathy, tossing Black
Hats in Montgomery, calls to reassemble, to fight
Evil unable to erase enough of us
Refusing to be blurred, we piece together

AAS 231

Instructor: Cynthia L. Dorsey
Journal Reflection: "What is race? When did I discover it?"

Daddy said
Look out for the white man
While he guided my eyes
To the man in brown trousers
Brown hair and blue eyes
Daddy said it was his disguise

Cuz blond hair
was too obvious
but daddy was too smart
to be fooled

He taught me to
squint my eyes and open my ears

Never let a white man know your fears
Never let a white man see you love
Never give him anything to strip you of
Only thing you show a white man
is how to stand
back held straight

I strutted just like Daddy
Black and mighty
Always with a bag of tricks
just for whitey

Right into school

RAY JANE

with a bad/Black attitude
Wanting nothing more than
to show and prove
Prove to Daddy what Black
could do
Prove to the white man
that I'm watching him too

When a white girl passed me by
I'd smile real slick-like and
cut my eye

that is, until one
smiled right back,
came on and over and gave
me some dap
I didn't quite know
what to do with that

So I asked her name,
said *what is your game?*
She smiled and replied
We're one and the same
I just wanted to see
if it could be
that my daddy was right
about black folk watching me

Black Thigh Thaumaturgy

These thighs are rude
They leave no space
Between
No option
But to be warmed
Conjuring best
When rubbed
Magic mentioned in
Barely uttered whisps
Air barely getting through
There
Ain't no gaps here
Their
Alchemy coming fast
Spouting sea
Sometimes slapping, clapping
Friction between bits
Chafing, creating fire
Exothermic reactions
Booming, My thighs
Stay moving
Even when still
The magic to birth
The magic
To kill

Black Econ

Hoovering my coins
You can tell I'm a pro

Pushing photons like physicist
I domesticate your logic
with this counterintelligence

Acknowledging you, debunking
destroying, bombing, playing coy
in courtrooms and conferences

I, Spook
Press select buttons to get you runnin'
Out N' gunnin', Black beret-in'
Cuz they comin'

Tryna get you to picture yourself
before they frame you, hem you up
like Santa Monica, like Pratt

Hunt you, like Martin,
when he wandered into wilderness, also
known as researching economic evidence
for why We have yet to claim Our excellence,
How the dollars don't add

Convince you that it's bad
to keep resources in our own community
to feed poor babies free breakfast, or sustain them
with sustenance from ground

BLACK LIKE THAT

Grow fresh fruit, in the ghetto
We Geppetto and don't even know

Starving, for more than liquor stores
and Starbucks that don't give a fuck
if we eat

Despite that, we spend recklessly. Come, go
on a journey with me Kin, call yo'self dollar
and I'll provide the skin, let's get clear
on how long you'll circulate here, can't make
a plan for you, until you understand the brevity
of your lifespan

Cuz if you Asian, you'd spend an average
of 28 days, in Asian hands, by Asian means

This is true ish, it would be 19, if you was Jewish

But nah, You a Black dolla. So no one hears you
holla, You evaporate quick. Not talking days,
I'm talkin' hours, in fact, I'm talkin' six

So sis, when you are pondering riches
or how abundantly to exist, make it stack,
bring it back, protect it, please mine yo' Black
businesses

Milepost 6

THOSE Bodies

"They say Black don't crack..."

Possession

Strange fruit swinging in my throat
it ain't my groan you hear
it ain't my rasp siphoning
bloodhound hollering in the trees
behind me

Naw, it aint mine

Not my snatched baby
still living on my placenta, not my
wailing mouth, pouring sorrow until
deafening

I told you, it aint mine

Can't claim deep scoff erupting
unapologetically from proud Moor
laughing in horror, as liberties lay
in the hands of those taught,
how to bathe

No, it aint mine

When love returns, finds itself in my mouth
gods unravel themselves
walk naked off my tongue, loud
and undeniable, proximity aside

Still, aint mine

Especially, while toes make shallow

BLACK LIKE THAT

tunnels into earth, life's current rooted
into my spine, flowers becoming from spirit
Magic high in the dew, early and wet
drops drum through sternum

what is conjured, is not mine

I am, borrowed
constructed by time
glass-blown vessel
seeing out of a shared experience

when creation possesses this body
I am no longer, mine

For the Black Body

Jaheim McMillan
armed with a Black   body
dared to exist in the sunlight

extinguished
well before he'd know
the reach of his legacy

taken, again

another rewritten history
where the innocent become
the enemy, again

Another Black   forever
reduced
to a body

And we
add
another name
to the tally
of Black
Men
slain
to distract us from the carnage
of capitalist gain

drag   chalk from
bottom to top
of a Black   life

reduce
us to
out lines

The other day
I saw Anubis
yesterday
I saw Anubis
Today
I saw Anubis
write a new name-
Keenan Anderson

against my better judgment
I lost count of the executions
I watched
again

Mind absent yet wondering
how I can still subject myself
to repetitive spiritual battery
who will I be
when the acrid acid of it's assaults
overloads my capacitor?

Starting to behave like I'm Pahvlov's
trigger warnings
Got Bull Connors dogs salivating
Taste for persecution
Solution to the Black problem

weighs the same as the
trauma in a Black body's
swing
a Black body's
last song
how it's often a scream

"I cant breathe!"
wails the same grim melody as

RAY JANE

"They tryna
George Floyd me!"

Death notes attempt to lull us
witnesses
back to sleep
other Black   bodies
to consider ourselves privileged
to still be
living
to be on this side of the cell phone screen
as if
we
aren't able to feel his anxiety, his terror
our faces cementing, inside battle is raging
mistaken for inability
to recall easily, easier
than many, how many times a day
this skin
recalculates
the likelihood of my survival

How *this*
 skin
demands that I clutch joy
with BOTH hands
cuz I'll never know when
I'll lose another Black   man,
Again
I choose to lift the Black   man
Again
cuz all the world can be a noose
to a Black   man
Again

So for you Black   man, again
Stolen Black   man
I snatch back your name

and return to you all of your breaths taken

| 50 |

For Sandra

I live in this Blackness,
convinced that I am cursed

Yet I,
touch as if my hands
were made of good magic

I see the reruns of we
strewn, beaten
dead for all to see

Glassy,
my eyes brim and waterfall into
deep, darkness
like my skin

I weep

For the brotha/brothas
sistah/sistahs
extensions of my humanity
Coincidentally, also, cloaked in my same/curse

Related by mortality
propensity to be slain
bound to each other, again

I reach for understanding

While my poor heart breaks
our society/ penniless coin

RAY JANE

immersed in a wealth of shame

I want to emblazon my white coat
with your name

Knowing even that
ain't white enough to save me
from being lain to unrest

May I protest?
But if I raise my hand
if I abduct

Must I also endure the consequences
of unprofessional conduct

I want to mourn you properly
coat my brownness in Blackness for you
take a break from healing them
to ponder why
no one halted to restore you

You refused
to apologize for your magic

My sistah, My sister, Mine

I weep for you, for our crime
our tears reflect the sentence
while the world foolishly awaits
the repentance of our owner's descendants

We, wise and exhausted
anticipate another

Wondering what's worse—
the penalty, or being called a curse

Daunte Wright

How heavy is your cross?

if X's always mark your spot, if
every where you stand has grave potential

when your death has siblings
only a few miles away
tell me   how   heavy?

Does it cut into your skin like mine do?
does its weight ebb and flow
but never quite   dissipate?

Help me?
What are you supposed to say?

while their mouths are full of excuses for accusers
while their mouths   are filled   with your blood

And yet

the heaviest part of it, the knowing
there is no monopoly on grief
that other souls also live under a stampede

Lord,
if this is all a dream
wake us up before they drop another
guillotine

| 53 |

Milepost 7

Wanted

WANTED

INFORMATION WANTED.

JEFFERSON DAVIS in company with his brothers Moses and Lewis, left London County Virginia, about eleven years ago in search of freed'm, but on their way they was attacked by slave-catchers, at which time a battle ensued, resulting in the capture of Jefferson, while the other two Moses and Lewis effected their escape; but since Jefferson has purchased himself and came to Canada.

Any one knowing any of the above named persons, will receive a reward of $5, by making the same known to the Rev. H. J. Young, Elder of the M. E. Church, Chatham, C. W.

Chatham, May 2nd, 1856.   3

Provincial Freeman and Weekly Advertiser (Windsor/
Toronto/Chatham, Canada West), May 10, 1856
"Rev. H. J. Young searching for Moses and Lewis Davis on behalf of Jefferson Davis [former enslaved man]," Provincial Freeman and Weekly Advertiser (Windsor/Toronto/Chatham, Canada West), May 10, 1856, Last Seen: Finding Family After Slavery, accessed May 3, 2023, https://informationwanted.org/items/show/1141

Blacker

Listen. Im only finna tell you again
I'm blacker than you thought
Real Black like that side of the hand
Blacker than you let me be
Blacker than you want
Blacker than your choke holds.
Blacker than your taunts
Blacker than black slave catchers
Blacker than your toms
Blacker than you can imagine
Real Black like that side of the hand
On that side Black!
I'm Blacker than you thought
Listen. I'm only finna tell you again

Mutiny

Here we be
death defying feats, tightroping an infinity
glorious, to say the least

we rise in heaps
following great Spirit
forward, onward, no kin to defeat

when killed continuously
no death could shake our feet
our hips mud-bricked, we concrete

we *are* the leap
pushing forward no matter
the fee— paying in blood, and *even* in dreams

we stay pressing on, through hydrant and teeth
we know from whom, this strength was bequeathed

So if yo' skin stays too brown, stand up on yo' feet!
If your lips were *once* considered too round
get your ass up and clap!

but won't you look at that!

the very thing *they* hated
and painted on us mid-contortion
they run to foreign to implant in the body
gaudy imitations, out of proportion

it's the closest the vultures will ever get to that

RAY JANE

fight me if it ain't a fact!
as a matter of tact,
I'll be polite and just let you hold dat.

and now we're back

and while the bombs are still falling over Baghdad,
we will the light to rise over Palestine

Great God piping through our gifts
articulating in various versions of Einstein
the roots of the genius are mine

telling the devil *now get thee behind!*

we reclaim our time, reclaim our minds

show the world, the gold isn't in our mines
but the deep connections we aim to find

noting first, that any crime against
the rich in wine deserves collective switch
boomeranged lash of the whip
to silence pseudo-massahs lying lips

we are *already* equipped
so rise and take back the ship.

Cutlass

I let my cutlass swing free
when I split the width
of invader's bush weed
I won't be kept from what has been
promised to me, answering the call of
granddaughter of the escaped into the trees
cut to the quick with this   understand this real quick
this some   warrior energy

Ancestral lifeboat, I
Returned to your chest when your body starts to bloat
gathered their villainous monikers
balled them up in back of my throat
Spit back serrated stars damned in sunken ships
chopped their bullets mid-air bend— Neyo helped me
Tip bows of boats until spouts reopened
Struck your sternum with butt of blade
'til you coughed out your code-switching religion
in the middle of your sentence

Reteach you not to call for white Jesus
while our bronze and woolied one listens
we one, and both amused
Always protecting you, look over your shoulder
saw the enemies name in Anubis's book
In spirit, we high-fived and told those foolish enough
Not to flee, to come against you, with me
At your back, *look alive   while you can   zombie*

brushing last residue of lies off your tongue
hate's halitosis neutralized

RAY JANE

get that scent   up off me   we still share skin
refused to be confused with those who
Stay consistent and unclear—
claim democracy   major in fear
save complexions that are easier to protect, then
pretend not to pull Black bodies out their teeth by the tendons

I'm at your back while you holla
Me and my ancestors never believed you!

Same way they claimed to save you, let a virus sweep through
In thick of death and darkness, I slipped to snip the bands
pulled down masks, so you, would see the real reason creep through
population control only works with less people
start with the poor   underrepresented
Baby they belly been full off the feeble

I keep my blade sharp for those of us still fetal
and go right back to playing cops 'n robbers
return to plunder the riches of others
though not surprising since we all know   the only cure
they know is war
just take a look at their medicine
destroy   living things for profit, easy to slither when slinging
snake   oil
teach   their healers nothing about remedies
of the   earth
instead   disconnect from the body, betray it with chemical con-
fusion   then
call the immune system disloyal

Armed with their caduceus
But you was born with the cutlass
Simultaneous identities demand you learn to hiss   like Hermes
And *blaspheme* like Thoth, herald the Bible, but
question what you're taught, remember you were
Uninvited to the selection of testaments,
easier to plagiarize that way
Lost Jesus in Ethiopia, looked for him in all their
mirrors and yet forgot his face

BLACK LIKE THAT

Thus, I return to your time to remind
You were born with a blade in the mind

Pump Action

It grates at me—the hate for me
Ripping at my seams, every time I see, Me
Pulled apart for all to see, still, killing me

I can't be the only one feeling fatigued, breath of life escaping me.
Where are the Gs?! The ones who cock glocks for the whole hood
to see. Why ain't y'all fools avenging We?! Why ain't We in these
streets?! Straight merkin'. While gentrifiers think it's safe to keep
lurking, rounding up our parts, bout to get these hands,
or at least, these ramparts

Are We smart? Unclear

Seeing as We remain under thumb. Made us believe
We not wine, We just squashed grapes of a people.
We weep under steeples and keep the burner at bay
like the way They dragging these Bodies is for play.

WWYD
Waiting to hear

what Yeshua has to say. Cuz my version ain't
eyes of blue, and bullshit excuses to keep me in line. *My* Yeshua
is rage, condemnation, feels a way, that They, don't even know His
name. Leviticus and Deuteronomy too cuz mines could also get slain
in these streets. Must be cuz *My* Yeshua is actually bronze and
wooly. No wonder we steady getting crucified

This ire lives outside time

Cuz I AM NOT okay! Placing peace and its bible

BLACK LIKE THAT

back to lay, next to my dreams. Again,
A time for prayer has gone away.
Time to mount up!

We done did that, pray shit, that march shit, that
turn the other...peace shit, that doing it your way shit.
Still, consoling our mothers while America drags its feet...shit.
Ain't nobody coming to save we...shit

Got white friends that rather be entertained by me than
tout their bravery, exercise that privilege for me. Put some
hands on Becky! *Especially*, if I'm barbecuing,
holding my skittles, or *just*, running on your street.
Keep your kin from calling the Klan on me.

What kinda ally moves like frenemy?
How could they sit by, perpetually watching
the end of me. Truth is, if you ain't riding for me
then *you* the enemy

So get to work!

Align with me, take up alms, combine with me
But nah, You rather stay tongue in cheek, than
brrattttt lips like mag. Shoot this silence up, with me!

I'm mad. I'm fucking livid. I'm beyond. Angry. How you so
restrained?! It was all merry when you could ignore my humanity
Again. *Oh yeah? You got Black friends?!* You 'bout to see just
how *that* kind of Black a friend can be, when the ancestors who
been drumming they're feet, get to
leapin'   jumpin'   up outta me

Better MOVE!

We got that wicked speed. Ask Carlos, John and Smith,
Tommie. Raising fists, like Toby right before amputation.

Tell   Gabriel to hold the horns.

This revelation, far from heavenly. In a nation hell bent on bending

| 63 |

RAY JANE

me, no lube...

Don't shoot!

The 1s with me. Y'all so silly, thinking we not finna collect this loot
We kick in the door, wavin' the 4-4, at 4-5, COVID, agent Orange

coughin, filling coffins   We
wonderin' how   We still   alive?

We warriors necromancin', We 'bout to rise!

It's 'bout to get live. The power
from which we derive, it's about to
arrive. Cuz we just sent for the nukes
while we the spooks Creep up in that
back door also known as ours

They   want   war

Kings and Queens begin to
quantemplate things, a problem
when we get to whispering. Start
turning off camera phones
and get to sharing messages with these feet
again. Stomping in our gumboots
you won't know who's who soon
waiting for our smoke
to rise, signal to reject compromise

Entranced, I reminisce on visits to
deep south, to deep Georgia, red dirt
clay in my mouth. My peach trees branching
into fists. Mad Handberry with my gifts
Spirit of great granny demanding
return of all parts of my fifths

Breaking open jail cells
recollecting my begotten, won't let you
let them go rotten

BLACK LIKE THAT

We plottin', planning on disrobing from these tainted American
garments. As Def Poet Preach(ed)- "The fabric of our lives" still
soaked in bloody fields of cotton

'Bout to get muddy buddy...
'cuz mamas people in here too, spirit of wild ass maroons

Jamaica has entered the room

Rastafari with Tech 9s and spliffs, mad Marley riffs. Talkin' loud
and sayin' nuff Black pride, no permit, refusing to be policed

Pulling up with machete–
Who's tryna get fleeced?!
Patois erupting from me, as I enunciate our saga– *Dem bways dem
dey MAGA!* But we a quick study, *Rise up til' dem shook mon,*
remember the Art of War, pages we took from Book-man
tryna get free like early Haiti– Jean-Jacques and Toussaint

gods return to haunt us, taunt us to action, reminding us
of back when, when we were stronger, when we were better.
Gotta get our moves together

Practice your capoeira!

Breaking the chains
bounding our brains we unfetter, change requires
kicking down the towers of the occupiers
Time to get all the liars!

Don't want to hear it! How the jury split, ain't nobody doin'
time. So it's time to reclaim our dimensions, and when it's
time to act up, make sure you get the frequencies you attract up
I wanna see all y'all despised, and chastised, the unauthorized
and colonized, get energized past your compromise
Tryna canonize the uncivilized.

Don't say shit
or look for It, It won't be televised. Get these war cries
harmonized. Don't be so mesmerized by what *they* prize.
When your existence is already so minimized, why

RAY JANE

are you even afraid to die?

Stop stuntin'
Don't ask me nuttin'
When you see me runnin'
Just get your shit together
And decide
Are you comin'?

Milepost 8

The Duty of the Hunted

"A hit dog will holla…"

He Was in His Alt-Right Mind

For those lost like Buffalo.

A white supremacist went to market, again
to hunt Black targets, but the story got misinterpreted
as a racially-motivated mass shooting cuz terrorism takes effort
calculating Black death takes work, for example
how many bullets makes a food desert, only
supermarket in the community

we guess, if you can't shoot 'em, at least
starve the ones that got free
just add them Black bodies to the tally like...
10 dead, 3 injured, 3 in the parking lot, 9 in the market
11 Blacks, 2 whites, what a shopping list must look like
to a terrorist, oops I think I said it again

A white supremacist went to market, again
to hunt Black targets, but the story got misinterpreted
missing the mark, a reporter remarked on
a Black survivor's calm, the retelling
again, distorted, eyes glazed and dancing off into the distance
face devoid of reaction, each word with slight taste
of disbelief, what is obvious has to be translated
if you don't look like me

Black trauma must be, a different dimension of being
she was not calm, she was   trauma in action, in pre-grief
in the post-apocalyptic   ictal   state   following the seizure
that is white supremacist ideology

A white supremacist went to market, again

to hunt Black targets, but the story got misinterpreted
called this uncaged beast crazy
tried to explain away that unchecked rage of hate
often leads to Black death, via white rampage by design
He was in his alt-right mind!

Powers that be re-conditioning, with every   thing   to   gain
by   shifting   narratives
making every hate   criminal   crazy, until it's tradition
and the penalty is lawfully made null
oh wait...that's already possible

A white supremacist went to market, again
to hunt Black targets, but the story got misinterpreted
hunting, must be every season
when concealing wickedness, there's always a reason
psych!   just   recalculating
2 firearms purchased legally
2 minutes we Twitched   while no siren blared
watched   handcuffed madman handled with care
ENOUGH!   to make a target forget who's the threat here

A white supremacist went to market, again
to hunt Black targets, but the story got misinterpreted
why aren't politicians open in discussing white supremacists?
but we know conflicted interests won't let the vicious
demonize their kin, when we might see them
for what they've always been—the culprits
feign horror, each May we go on counting
Black bodies blocked from budding, bad spring

WHEN A WHITE SUPREMACIST GOES TO MARKET
AGAIN
we the targets grow tired of pretending, smiling at day jobs
while Black lives keep ending
soon, the bow won't tolerate no more bending
soon, if our blood remains in the street
white supremacists might meet targets
who won't turn the other cheek
who'll be past the point of reinterpreting

Politikin'

I don't know shit about politics

Oh, but if you ask me whose video was the illest
and who's rhyme style is the realist, *Yeah,* I could tell you dat.
Politics though? *Nah,* I don't know shit bout dat

I don't care about Bush(s) in Iraq, or the funds that we lack
But I could tell you there ain't no war on crack
No recently passed act, to make a liberal or a republican
Give a damn about my international ties
Or should I say, my lack thereof

Cuz even though they stand, and proclaim
on anything dot gov, that the sky's my limit
They never hesitate to trim it— that is
my connection to a way, to realize these dreams they claim
are not deferred

Sometimes I catch a political address
Listenin' for any word, indication to me that one day
We'll have tv in every classroom, enough trumpets
to make a band, neighborhoods, that don't fume with
toxic waste plants

Genetically engineered ants who come
Bite lil' Ray Ray and Shay Shay, and give
them some type of cancer
That aint covered by Medicaid

Yeah, maybe then I won't hover, around the fact that
anything Black still has a negative connotation, and the majority

of the soldiers stationed overseas, have Jackson and Ruiz
for last names

Maybe then I won't call it a shame, when the constitution
can be used "to tap my cell and my phone in the basement
and federal agents..." are mad, cuz them phones ain't been on
since your daddy got laid off from Walmart

America ain't got no heart, the blood pumpin' through its veins
been tainted for centuries, by national and international enemies
Whose interests always find a way, to creep over the citizen
take a squat, lay something foul, and still be found innocent

Yeah, I just love how nothing we own is owned by us

And how the "in God we trust" ain't backed by gold so,
the ink gets a little bit more faint every day. How public school
is like boarding school, you know, just without the funding
tiny bit of Fahrenheit-48-ing the book list

How my grandpa is still working, at the tender age
of seventy-three, holding on to me, for dear life,
'cuz his social security check is about twelve dollars,
but his prescription is just over fifty...thousand

Yeah son, I heard it through the grapevine, that monopolies
are just fine, that the people outside the U.S. need jobs,
more than we do. And you too, can get the cure for AIDS & cancer
if you got the dough boo

And if you didn't know, the best way to get re-elected
is to take the niggas you rejected, and try to sign their language
on a public service message

They won't remember how you never heard one single sigh
covered up every single lie, with a white girl cry, a kente tie
That you could loosen, when the sin choked too much

Yup! Everyday my wallet gets a little fucked–
Bushonomics costs more than Reaganomics,
we can't tell the difference between an Arab and a Sheikh,

BLACK LIKE THAT

place them all under Muslim terrorist heading

I'm too busy on the streets, stealin' purses to pay for
college tuition, sellin' dope to keep from sniffin', livin'
dirty so I won't miss a sweet kiss from my babies, 'cuz I'm off
in the navy dodging bullets not meant for me

What we haven't learned from slavery–
A lesson to look around at your own shit
The poverty, the pain, five year old girls aspirin' to dance
in videos, internet-gangstas tryna steal my right to prose

Tryna get a history lesson, on every page that's not ripped out,
African American Studies program, that hasn't been phased out
Tryna find my mom & pop store that they closed down, so some
fucking corporation could keep us all down

Watching the destruction of everything that I love, with audacity,
when you clearly see my eyes are filled with tears, How America
has been systematically fucking me all these years. What's
private bleeds and my womb falls free, legislation finally
aborting me

You ask me why I don't watch politics on tv? Why I haven't
kept up? I look up, eyes as cloudy as a monsoon
Give you the finger, so you know what to do,

Tell you simply—

I been too busy watching my soul die to vote, watching
my baby choke on industry smoke, watching
the jails fill with all my mans-an-nem, who sold you
what you supplied

As the penitentiary becomes an industry, and all my Black
babies get sucked in. When brown people barely make up 30%
of the land, And 90% of us end up with shackles about our wrists
Again!

Yeah son,
I know exactly why all the charges stick

RAY JANE

Why the senate and house of reps are still filled with hicks
Why all the fortune 500 companies are still run by dicks
And right before the channel flicks

You try to tell me,
I don't know shit about politics.

Georgia's On My Mind

Raise your hand if you're surprised
numb to the bull those at bottom bat no eye

we been bathin' in American lies
y'all come on in now, ain't y'all the ones that said
the water was fine?

for it seems, patriotism just took a piss on the American dream
Headlines saying crazy things, odd phrases like
"American democracy"

we guffaw at the hypocrisy,
as if democracy ever needed an adjective for it to live, unless
it was
never meant to be free

wait...shhh...according to CNN correspondents
another headline said "rioters unleashed"

final piece to dark truths erupting in deafening tweets

which American Eagles are these?!
who's mans is this? We ask to those clothed in privilege
that's yo' people? Nah?
cuz they just set some shit on fire, yelling that it was your steeple

they throwin' tantrums cloaked in coups, crappin' on everything
like babies do, so easy to name them *they,* but *they*
look like you

where Maury at?! Cuz every time they sue, we 99.9% percent sure

| 75 |

RAY JANE

they daddy is *you*

so allies please! get yo' kids!

wait...shhhh...just scrolled up and saw the most ridiculous
game of cops and robbers, but I couldn't tell who
was who

nuff shouting bout law and order, cuz Capital Hill lookin' real
HBCU-ish. Quick!

somebody call the authorities, they got a minority in the senate!
hol' up...wait sis...that's just the republicans. It's
getting real interesting, in a way that only mirrors do

America, you betta pull down your slip sis! The whole world
is watching you, wondering how it feels to find out you're
a cannibal

when the full moon rises over this land, and
the hungry are revealed as animals. When Black WAP
revives you again, them drums sound,
in the key of Abrams

the unsullied rise in this winter, answering anti-ANTIFA's
with their own Warnock, wondering how a government
can claim to protect
when they can't 'eem keep the door locked?!

those born in the space between aperture and the floor,
oiling the hinges of that swinging door rise to traverse and
reclaim our frames. Standing by, standing down

while hate makes plain, that God shall not be mocked
we watch, we sit, real still, unable to untwist grill,

when nooses and rubber bullets,
finally become de-escalation drills

when there ain't enough Black lives to kill, the blue hue
starts looking real ill. In the chaos, the not yet numb shout

BLACK LIKE THAT

for relief from bills,

demanding those with continuous muttering of myths provide,
the evidence for evaporated racism, in the clear
presence of uncanny arrogance
the likes of which, reverberates through this American skeleton.

Shell-shocked, polls come apart like sea, the people
casting votes to invoke
The Barbary— pirating the hopes of White Supremacy

Hilariously, the blind scream, horrified
as their masks shattered for all to see

super spreaders sounding real su-per pre-da-tor-ish to we
got mayor Brandon Scott like *"shorty...pull ya mask up"*
you're coughing up all our glory

conspiracies on ventilators too, *"people dyin' shorty"*
wondering what we're being distracted from, while
they out their playing coup

but like I said in the beginning, raise your hand if you shocked
betta yet, raise your hand if you not

Privilege

* Quotes taken from speeches by Martin Luther King Jr entitled: "I Have A Dream" and "The Other America"

Privilege is slippery, not easy to grasp it seems
privilege is just beyond the reach of most minds, *they*
find it too hard to conceive, that *they* could live on top of *we*

how the design of that truth could be so well-woven
into America's seams, they get so confused they
even use the wrong quotes to justify their means

BLM hit the streets and every major corporation started quotin'
MLK Jr, but somehow, amidst the wall between proceeds
and privilege, they managed to miss the dream

Amazing, around January 15th, "allies" start thoughtlessly
saying things, like, let us be judged
Quote- by the content of your character - end quote

Y'all sounding like parrots, when it's clear it has been a while
since the morality of this continent was rich in anything
but laments held in submission

with presumed derision, the very greed that aimed to assassinate
the vision, is licking chops, like it's waiting for permission
But, we recall,

that the definite distance between us and history as told,
by Gepetto, is exactly the length of lies that lie just beyond
the tip of what we can sense

BLACK LIKE THAT

Quote- but we refuse to believe the bank of justice
is corrupt- end quote

If hate was the bad check that America produced to cover its debt
then the superstition of race must have signed it. The truth
of the Dream came later–

King, speaking from within the wilderness, tried to
challenge the thing dangerously demanding:

Quote- confronting our nation until there is an honest
conversation with it- end quote

If we are going to build a person by their words, let's not
mince them and hide the hands of hired men, distraction,
from the truth is the sickness in it

how would you react, if the facts suggested ain't no difference
between rights and privilege, but the definition, was edited
by Jim's Crows who stand to make a profit off the sale
on the latter of those

interesting aside

if you put "privilege" in the thesaurus, what is offered is
prerogative

but let's not get off topic...

ah yes, we were talking about placing privilege across the tracks
claiming you have to have the right to live close to that
we all been hacked, been stuck up in this shell, since the plan
was hatched

If you really want to honor Dr. King, quote "The Other America"
and see how quick a bullet can kill fact.

American Dream-Robbed

I ain't even askin' for nothin' crazy;

a passion lucrative enough that work
is a hobby. So I can stop buying scratch-offs and
talking to myself in slogans cuz "hmpf, you never know"
I just need a few mili'

I ain't even askin' for nothin' crazy;

just enough to negate financial chains
to break the lock on freedom
to have it defined by something other than lack
take all my niggas to Webster's crib,
wondering why he ain't never said nothin' good
about our mamas, we all got questions

I ain't even askin', for nothin' crazy;

just want to pay off my 2 houses of debt
the one I live in and the one American education
got me in the system with
the lie that's still accumulating interest

I ain't even askin' for nothin' crazy;

I won't even keep my riches to myself
I'd go on a grace tour and buss open every cage green money
can manage, release all my peeps from massah's heavy sole
squeeze my money between our necks and
the bottom of America's boots
the ones   we got   with no straps

BLACK LIKE THAT

I ain't *even*   askin'   for nothin'   crazy;

Pay all my niggas' biggest bills of sale
then tell them crackas not to look for we,
buy our disappearance from hell
build the boat back and sail off the grid, maybe
we'd rebuild the underground railroad on the sea
get wifi, tell all our niggas "you can ride for free"   this time

I ain't even askin' for nothin' crazy;

some bills I'd save in the trust
between my mattresses, yo momma's granny's bank,
then, spend the lasts of my millions, on land. I would
return me to my folk's moorish ways, cultivate gardens,
by choice this time. I'd have me, a field *full* of blackberries,
the edible kind– grown strong and never plucked too early.

I ain't even askin' for nothin' crazy;

though one could always argue, this flesh been on the menu
I'm just trying to change the ingredients in America's kitchen
get me and mine off the blocks
no more choppin', no more auctions, just the capitol, to start

I ain't even askin' for nothin' crazy;   just a refund.

Milepost 9

Inquiry

INQUIRY

MR. EDITOR—I wish to inquire brother Anthony. He belonged to Elias Hodges, of Barber county. Alabama. He was with a lawyer named Seals, in Clayton, Barber county, Alabama, the last time I saw him—about 20 years ago. I do not know what name he goes by now. His mother's name was Jennie: she belonged to Green Neeley. I belonged to Elias Hodges and was called Little Berry, as there were two Berrys on the place. Sister was sold to Jno. D Johnson as well as I remember; she also belonged to Green Neeley, and was sold with her husband, Phillip Johnson—her name was Martilda. I will pay for any information that can be given of my brother or sister. My address is Millican, Texas.

BERRY NEWTON.

Southwestern Christian Advocate (New Orleans, LA), September 9, 1880

"Berry Newton searching for his brother Anthony," Southwestern Christian Advocate (New Orleans, LA), September 9, 1880, Last Seen: Finding Family After Slavery, accessed May 3, 2023, https://informationwanted.org/items/show/4497

Name– the first displacement

This name
is supposed to be home

Supposed to be, a place to return to
instructions on how to recall oneself

But this name, sits atop this skin,
this skin, has been homeless

Since it crossed the sea. My name,
somewhere lost in the Atlantic— drowned

No wonder I choke, when trying
to pronounce myself, why I stutter

When attempting to expound, on myself

A wonder, that I know me at all
when missing, original definition

The depth of me, thus, immeasurable,
but then, I guess, that was by design

Unknown

an unmarked grave walking
a bank for bullets redeposited in their
intended targets, for you
I write, I speak, I proclaim your name

unknown, a dead Black man
an unmarked grave, dig into the dirt

thrown on your name, the dirt you did not earn
mistaken for the depth of your skin
I write, for you

repurposed body, with spirit trapped inside
unaware your enemy stay strapped
or that you, stay in his hairs
no victim, you deserve a name
a home— the first place to belong
perpetual threat of being undone
demolished, gentrified existence, another statistic
you are more than a blip on graph, exponential
even in death, I mention you with intention

unknown, a dead Black man
an unmarked grave, never a slave

but smelted metal caged your memory
all the same, I am your papers
get free, between the words I speak
your name, build you a mansion
in which we reminisce

RAY JANE

tell the story of how a wave, unsolicited
by the wrong woman
gets you ditched, how your life was lost
like loose cigarettes, on the block they still blare
loosies!, and I see you fighting Lucy,
devil in a blue badge
got you breathless again

unknown, a dead Black man
an unmarked grave, becoming jazz on my page

I close my eyes, immerse in your music
fill the mind with smoke and shadowed lighting
spotlight your plight in the middle of the only
stage you graced, before jealousy given too much
responsibility, bent your Black and brass body to wailing,
too much revolution in you, you blew like a French horn

partial to your darker works
I wonder aloud *how could a thing dying so
loud, be silenced*

I am your permission, the answer to your
pleadings for rescue
never let them forget you
shifting the burden of proof
they murdered you,
made us careful with what we named ourselves,
because that's all that's left of you

unnamed, a splinter in the mind, we shall not forget

in this life, you were poorly worshiped
too many humans made altars
the worth of a Black man's richness depends
on who their God is
too blasphemous, killers know no creator
so they could not make you

unknown, a dead Black man or
an unmarked grave

Churning

stewing in the deepest pain
my skin recalls the lash
each time someone asks
how many times?

the too slow separating
of epidermis
against tightening rope
wakes me from sleep
when I consider impossible
thoughts
like
sons

lost
to white cotton
when inked into law,
shouting
get your niggers here!
they're on discount now

drown me
in the last wisps of purple
left in my incantations
when returning me
became a threat

terror tangled in my
memory of mammy, I mean
momma, you mean
mammy, I mean

INFORMATION WANTED OF MY SON, Allen Jones. He left me before the war, in Mississippi. He wrote me a letter in 1853 in which letter he said that he was sold to the highest bidder, a gentleman in Charleston, S. C. Nancy Jones, his mother, would like to know the whereabouts of the above named person. Any information may be sent to Rev. J. W. Turner, pastor of A. M E. Church, Ottawa, Kansas.

"Nancy Jones seeking information about her son Allen Jones," The Christian Recorder (Philadelphia, PA), May 20, 1886, Last Seen: Finding Family After Slavery, accessed May 3, 2023, https://informationwanted.org/items/show/834

RAY JANE

reverence

the prowlers remain
taunting history
growing more brazen
with what they burn

God, no longer, enough

I-dentities

I
I am
I am Black
I am Black
Woman

I
I am
I am Black
I am Black
Woman
Daughter

I
I am
I am Black
I am Black
Woman
Daughter
Sister

I
I am
I am Black
I am Black
Woman
Daughter
Sister
Auntie

I
I am
I am Black
I am Black
Woman
Daughter
Sister
Auntie
Cousin

I
I am
I am Black
I am Black
Female
Daughter
Sister
Auntie
Cousin
Friend

I
I am
I am Black
I am black
Female
Daughter
Sister
Auntie
Cousin
Friend
Neighbor

I
I am
I am Black
I am Black
Female
Daughter
Sister
Auntie
Cousin
Friend
Neighbor
Student

I
I am
I am Black
I am Black
Female
Daughter
Sister
Auntie
Cousin
Friend
Neighbor
Student
Doctor

I
I am
I am Black
I am Black
Female
Daughter
Sister
Auntie
Cousin
Friend
Neighbor
Student
Doctor
Love

I am
Love
Always

I
Am
BLACK.

Milepost 10

Are They Not Pastorals?

"You're either in or out, y'all lettin' out all my air..."

Sharecropper's Grands

Sharecropper blood/ coursing unpaved roads/ passing by fields of cotton and smelling despair/ cousins telling of summers dipped in old work, sunrise meets sunset amidst freshly bloodied calluses/ thirst strikes hot as Georgia heat/ red clay caked with reconstruction promises/ the singing removes the honey from their old flesh trumpets/ the cost too high to make it make sense/ My father invites me to let cotton draw new blood/ do what my ancestors died doing?/ I say no/ but forget the same way they did/ moonshine tipping at sunset/ open spout, passing itself to each speaking experience/ *ughhhhh thassit right there*/ burning/ I smile it down/ too ashamed to be weak in front of them/ breaking easy like hot water cornbread/ pretending I can hold mine.

Cotton

On my way to grandma's house
winding down roads that invented darkness
Georgia red clay grinding beneath us

On my way to grandma's house
the pecan groves leap to taste the sky
reaching for each other in rows
a human calls them perfect

On my way to grandma's house
we pass the white church first
know we are near to home, but not quite there
Mt. Zion Baptist, the final evidence
also, where the asphalt runs out

On my way to grandma's house
when farms that looked more like fields
I told Daddy to pull over right quick
I never seen the cotton so high

On my way to grandma's house
Daddy told tales of summer allowances
earned picking our ancestors nemesis
something old in my soul turned over

On my way to grandma's house
the reality of sharecroppin' in these bones
crept between me and my Daddy

On my way to grandma's house
he suggested I touch this snow white fluff on a stick

RAY JANE

I was mesmerized by how ugly hatred can make
something so beautiful
something so miraculous
something like the earth, growing our modesty

On my way to grandma's house
I refused to touch, Daddy nodded knowing,
also feeling what is still wailing
what remains bloodied in capitalism's farm

On my way to grandma's house
we agreed, our people have picked enough
cotton

Long Blood

*After "My Father Teaches Me about the Bees" by Joy Priest

This country's fauna, built through our long blood
seeps, We are silt

We are harvest, eroded
once wealth
farmed by hands, picked clean

When We — The Organics
weed,
We parse, reveal land-disturbing human
activities

Reduce a mountain to concrete,
shackle single bodies,
making mass graves

We— buried shadows, strange
to displace, soil, disrespectful ritual

We twist to the light,
examine Our own fruit,

finding
no faults, We uproot
wickedness branching in our fate

We open, bloom
in darkness, We peel our petals
to exalt the true sun

RAY JANE

We,
lowly blades of grass
We, fields of jasmine, perfume

survival, the original cotillion
tossing bouquets of trinity
gifting our thirsty stems

We wet Earth with
Promise of resurrection

Healing in Fields of Yarrow

"Yea,
though I walk through the valley of the shadow of death
I will fear no evil"

I will reject all energies coming for my neck,
including mine, if it's coming while I'm twisted up inside

I, forgot how to hide, once whipped so much I grew a hide
covered myself in *yes, I'm fine*s, though, the fee for growth neva'
lied, confide my truth, stack it so high in my excuses I nullify

Return to ancient working of the dirt, pick the burdock roots
to sweep the rotten fruit, long fallen from branching potential

on my Misty Copeland, I spin broom through cobwebbed
talents long unseen, venturing deeper into the thick of me,
my moss facing north, my riches, somehow, still green

panting in my own breath, I stop by my rivers to drink, lean
against myself while dipping into my own well, astonished
to find enough wet left to quench

this parchment finally moistened again, bits of me yet
broken creek moving along in me, we, recall the yarrow might
stop the bleeding, picking a few more than I need, sprinkling
in some fireweed
so much returning, in the wounds allowed to breathe
why we eat so much plantain finally making so much sense to me

got so lost in my recovery, startled, walked right into a fence
I forgot about this moat, this incessant layering of onion

RAY JANE

I'm peeling my traumas from my skin, sometimes
taking some skin with it
but thanking great Orisha for leaving the black intact

placing balm of Olodumare all over this back
pushing God deeply into these lashes, no wonder I fled
who runs toward pain so steep it stands you past straight into
back bending, posture of openly weeping, *nay,* violently wailing

with the spoiled ire of this creature, with creator,
for, sacrificing me to circumstance
why, the fare for better got to be so steep?
stretching this spine requiring realignment so
intent on the heavens, the weight of my mind
is allowed to unwind, chin points us in the direction

completion, body moving forward with two out of three
eyes still focused on where I've been, balancing
the weight of forward thinking, all the while knowing
the speed of destruction remains just a hair
faster than the healing

nearly reassembled at the edges of this version of me,
these equations somewhat resembling, peering out across my
scabbing scapes, trauma valleys finally filling with their water

no longer hydrostatic, my, whole biome returning to movement
healing, releasing joy to its natural state of acrobatics
grace, rising at dawn singing life's supreme mathematics

Moratorium

My moratorium's
an algorithm of rhythm and blues,
singing Ella in my belly
gumboots in my shoes

Movin' like mercury
but don't get confused
my style's mad, the type that
might blow a fuse

Got no choice but to go
'cuz I am the fuel
solution to the problem
'cuz I am the school

My people stop your sobbin'
it's time to get to mobbin'
the change that we are due
costs more than what they paid for you

Screaming

A great oak, sent a root forth to tell the truth
She spoke with the authority of an original—

We, know nobody tells you
the pain of the butterfly within her cocoon

We, keep the secrets of all creatures
nourish your death back to generations in soil

We, fill all lungs with our breath
bear witness to all methods of survival, constant like change

Your story books left out one thing– the screaming
the sound a soul makes enraptured in metamorphosis

We, listen
*as what makes the caterpillar too soft **stiffened***

We, bond branches and brace against banshee wailing
send mercy to her hanging limb as she, grows wings

We, breathe collective sigh of relief
when she finally fights herself out of what it takes to change her

We, rustle our leaves
when her enemies threaten to feast upon her progress

We, cringe at the screech of cracking chrysalis
sound of a lesson grating against petrified belief systems

We, cheer when courage echoes into her chest

BLACK LIKE THAT

while, what was left delicate stretches into twin mosaics, catches wind

We, exhale as collective
exchanging beauty for small silences to mute evolution's suffering

We,
tell the whole story in our rings, the book of life leaves out no pain

Milepost 11

"'Dese Women Altogether"/
Right Side Up Again

"...de fust woman God ever made was strong enough to turn de world upside down all alone..."

— Sojourner Truth,
Women's Convention,
Akron Ohio, 1851

Ain't I a Woman?

Ain't I a woman?
Though presumed voiceless,
I keep a fifth of Jack and
a lil' ditty on my tongue

Been marinating for years
in the salted brine of expectation,
I resound clear and un-pickled,
but best believe this pen
pisses vinegar, not easily ingested

Songs older than slave ships demand
my volume remains, at least
a howl in the wind, in the night
unladylike laced fingers about knickers
hiking my hems at any peon's
pejorative pleadings for my
silence,

*"my voice, and the voices
of women like me were not heard"**

So I become a wolf at twilight,
charge the night with my many throats

Open, vicious, vocal
And alive.

*Hooks, Bell. Ain't I a Woman (pp. ix-x).
Taylor and Francis. Kindle Edition

Brown

I sling this Melanin, like bags of   blow
So enchanting, they hate,   but   everybody know

This glow   grow, so   vine-like, So fine   like,
distance between Meandmajesty.   So bad
I be struttin', full   plume
everything fat like, no need to   zoom

leaving no doubt, no space,   no room
for nay say, the way I   play

these   adulting chords, symphony   of   cacophonous
melody, above   your   head, I   be   deep

buried   into the earth of your   existence
getting you together– repairing your   missense

no distance, comparable to my width,   the breadth of which,
coating you, warm, soft comfort food—   nourishment

Consumed,   and yet,   endless

don't try, you can't comprehend this, just put your hands out,
submit, and take in this doling   out   of my   gifts

now that you've been blessed don't get too   comfortable,
starting to rest on my morals, leaning heavily   on my peace

misperceiving the lingering of your honey   on my   lips
for excuse not to get that ass dismissed   *chile you   wish!*

RAY JANE

I'd bend this, favor in your direction,   but   I do not
commit, without proper   inspection

cuz every temple ain't worth my prayers, and I'd   rather not
have your pillars come down around my fears, *no   thank you*

I'll just as soon, gather up this gorgeous loom— remnants of
my colors, threading their way back   to   Oshun

I vacate, with my spirit intact, the Black on my back   not
tainted by wack attempts to emulate   my great

contrary to stories told of late, imitation does   not   flatter
sounding more like words spit by   mad   hatter

Foolishness   feigning as   mana,   my realness,
predating McCoy, so bye boy   with that   nonsensical lie

I   know   who   I   am

goddess   queen   creator,   weakness of men
dipped   for perfection, in   just   enough   melanin

Four Women Flying

*After Four women flying, without shoes/or wings- Bluest Nude: "Detail from 'Poem After Betye Saar's The Liberation of Aunt Jemima'"

by Ama Codjoe

Me and my girls go flying every other night
glass of wine or scotch, or gin if she from New Orleans
earth offerings roll themselves, minds expanding
as sunset ignites at ends of spliffs

We go baby
We climb into each other's rocket ships
communicating with our futuristic ear pieces
all in agreement, that perspective would be
the fuel for all of our voyages

Finally free to roam the realms untethered by
the earthly binding of skin, we rise into the limitlessness
of this molecular two-step
growing tentacles as we go

HOLLA

I'm slightly aware of my feminine appeal
I'm tryna
Ease my way into this swagger
Like hard work, on a hot summer day

I'm not tryna
incite heat stroke, not tryna kill folk
With this, *gat dayum,* this
good googa mooga, this
call on him! This shout
hallelujah!

So I
Try, oh how I try
to keep these
hemlines down by the knee
See,
these thighs'll get a rise
from most men, get 'em
walking and talking
Up, from mute and lame

There ain't no shame in this shape!

You gon' need
a whole lot more thread,
and a whole lot more tape,
to cover these curves,

you see
I swerves

| 108 |

BLACK LIKE THAT

on the skinny opposition,
they ain't in no position
to step against this
grown and sexy miss, just
too majestic, to be your mistress

you can miss this, with all them kiss kiss
sounds you makin'— that dog whistle
bound to get you
the bitch you callin' for
The confused low self-esteem, no-count chick
you steady, fallin' for

You ought to draw
a sign, or sketch a clue

'Cuz the quality you seek is right
in front of you

I'ma keep, doing me
and you gon' keep, thinking you
came up with the colors in your
plume, on your own
When I'm the reason you rock what you
rock, and flaunt what you got on

It's in attempt to get got by me

I set the tone
And the rules are changing—
You gon' have to step up your game
to keep on hang-ing, 'round these parts
gon' have to restart, get back to the part
of the game, when you called me
my name, instead of out of it

Where commitment
wasn't just a state of mind
and you couldn't just
snap out of it

RAY JANE

When a sista
could be woo-ed
would be courted

When the steps to gettin' down
were slower, and you were so rich
in integrity, that you could afford it

When we slow danced, instead of grinded
And you minded, if I walked on
the outside of the sidewalk

And we'd talk
'cuz my intelligence, was just as elegant
as my lovely scent

And you'd never let it be
That anyone could know me
better than you do

When you'd mind your manners
Shit, when you had manners in you

When no social media could break us,
'cuz you kept your mouth shut
about us, our fight was our fuss
and our laundry dried inside

Just tryna get back
to when you treated me
like the queen I be, like a lady
deserving of a *kang*, And not just
that thang

Way back when,
niggas were not lost boys
who didn't know the seeds that they let grow
or raise them to be crude, to disrespect
their women, and for profit, parade
their paradise in the nude

| 110 |

BLACK LIKE THAT

I'm just sayin'
Can I get your ear?
Can I remind you who you were
in yesteryear?

Know it's tough to hear, but I want you
Back robed in you greatness
I ain't just hatin', my Nubian
Where are my handsome
Black and proud gentlemen?

Not man bashin'
Not takin' out my emotional nines and
blastin', but really
I'm just askin'

Black Love

Your pain
speaks, describes to me
how you feel incensed

You open,
I put both hands on your misery
let them sink into
its clouds

your tears
condensing on me
I rub them into my skin
let them hydrate me

we are both afraid

you share
with me, the terrors
the things that go bump
in the night

or the day
or the morning
or the afternoon

how They
are always after me
and after you

tell me
you would never, could never

BLACK LIKE THAT

dip your magic into their
tantric traps

for fear
of false allegations, for
being colored, and you don't mean
Black, but exactly because of that

you don't
want to be Emmett Till'd
you don't want to be
killed

so you
lay your head back
back into my bosom
I rub your scalp

pick out
the things in your head
the things that flail
the things that are dead

we hold
hands tenderly, you quiet
your anguish, just long enough
to talk to me, to listen to me

you hear
me, you let me know
that I am
real

is this what Black love
is supposed to feel like?
it's so foreign
it don't feel right

But something
quantum leaps
from my simple reality

RAY JANE

Love explains,
you are more special to me
then I think you ever knew
and I don't take heed from you

I wear
my vulnerability like I ought to
flapping in our wind behind me
tied around my neck

making us
Super, sayin'
I love you, I need you
I want you to exist

you can't
be snuffed, if you die
I'll get cuffed, for you

real forever penchants
position ourselves
for prayer, us two

ponder each other's
safety

this intimacy
feels like silent vows, like me and you
might have jumped the broom
in a past life

might have
ran through the woods
holding hands, with hounds
at our heels

when we,
hid under floor boards
together

BLACK LIKE THAT

when we,
swam back
across the Atlantic

when my,
arms were tired
you put me on your back

when we,
cry salty tears
until our feet get back
in our sands, on
our original beaches

when we,
return to paradise together
we smile, realizing the same tribe
awaits us

we arrive
naked, waiting
to be re-robed
in our greatness, again

I weep,
you hold me
tilt my chin back to sky
place my headdress

I shine
your chest
with the earth, our earth
wipe a bit in lines under your eyes

hand you
your spear, instinctively
you toss it into air
yelling something guttural

mouth recalling
tongues stolen from you

| 115 |

RAY JANE

and I sing

I sing
our stories, old griots standing
tall in my throat

you kiss
me beneath mud brick love
we make ourselves, again

under first
place the stars were named
I call out yours, as passion so long-
poisoned, runs clean in our veins

our moans
our sorrow, escapes back
into the sky
our spiritus slowing

sweating beads
of forever, drenching the hide you
capture for me

herbs and
berries, smear on bellies
until I am swollen again
re-birthing us

gritting our
teeth, you mimicking me for
solidarity as I push out
the best of we

We deliver
A star, whispering to your heart
I remember you
I always will

My Black Is

My Black
is more
more than bondage and
bandaged dreams

my Black
is more
more than halted visions
of dastardly things

my Black
is more
more than hood
protagonists on tv screens

my Black
is more
than burning crosses
and military grade bullying
my Black

is
more
than slave movies
as singular Black narratives
my Black

is
old school jams
jammin' on Sunday mornings
my Black

RAY JANE

is
blue magic shining
betwixt
brand new braids

is
beads clacking
like carefree childhood
kinda

is
folded, undisclosed amount
tucked neatly in warm
grandma
palm

is
instinctive twitch
with mere mention
of belt or switch

is
collard greens with smoked
neck
bone
on shopping list

is
knowing which aunt got
the bomb
mac 'n cheese

is
moisture greedy
crown
wave caps
curls
mistaken for naps

is

BLACK LIKE THAT

knowing look between
strangers with familiar melanin

is
eye contact with that same
new friend
when THEY
start wilin'
my Black

is
pulling up
getting out
and giving greetings

is
cocoa butter scent
basketball
battlefields
and open hydrants

is
blues
jazz
funk
soul
drums
throat
the foundations of music

my
Black is
hidden like
Betthoven genius
behind all your
favorite
inventors

is
the cool
everyone is

RAY JANE

chasing

my Black
is
precious resource
the whole world
is
wasting

the fact is
this Black is
no longer
for
sale.

ACKNOWLEDGEMENTS

First and foremost I give all honor and gratitude to God, I can do anything with you. Thank you to my loving parents who encouraged my creativity, listened to millions of terrible poems, and who yell loudly for me when my voice falters. Momma, I know love because you *are* love. Dad, The Dad, you once told me the only thing I ever have to do is stay Black and die, thank you for that fact. Thank you to my brother, my grandparents, my extended family of aunts, uncles, and cousins— your love for me keeps me covered. Only my family could show me what it means to be Black, proud AND fly!

Shout out my beloved best friends, your love was integral to this process! Thank you for being my sounding boards, who I go to when I need to hash life out until it makes sense. Thank you for putting up with all my inquiries, book title changes, crying spells, and all manner of madness that comes with creating. Thank you for never allowing me to rush myself, or to minimize the positive impact that I already have on the world. I thank you all for rooting me, for not letting me settle, and challenging me to be brave in my dreaming. My words find safety in you and I am so grateful to God for friends who come with well water in hand. Anything you need, you know who got you.

Special thanks to my writing tribe, my poetry peoples, mi genté. To my sister in words Alexis Jackson, your help editing this book was critical. I know that God put you in my life to bless me toward completion! I will forever cherish the opportunity our sessions created for much-needed sistah-girl fellowship, returning to what we know about ourselves, and healing what the words could not. Shout out to the incomparable Peggy Robles-Alvarado who continues to cultivate spaces

ACKNOWLEDGEMENTS

that braid beings together. My deepest gratitude to my reviewers, who poured through my words with eagerness and gifted me the most gracious feedback: Bendi, Baba Ngoma, Roz, Elemen2al, Elizabeth (Lizzie) Strauss, La Bruja, Jane Spoken Word, Stacy Dyson, and the wildly talented Shockie G! Thank you to *all* my poetry family for showing me what it means to create in community. Thank you for the evenings and Sundays sacrificed to help me to be my best. Thank you for the text messages, the "yassss girl thassit" exclamations, the words that only poets could pen to push me. You have woven your way into my heart and I thank you for your handiwork. There are not enough letters in the dictionary to express how honored I am to know you, I hope that *thank you* will suffice.

I would also like to thank *Snarl: A Journal of Literature and Art* for first publishing "A Bop for Ketanji" in their "Online Exclusive Series" for August 2023 and Stacy Dyson & Co for publishing "Possession" in *TESORO: 1st Anniversary Firesingers.*

Lastly, I want to send a special thank you to all of *you!* Thank you for taking the time to read my book. Thank you for being willing to take a chance with me. I hope that you found yourself somewhere in my humanity, I am honored to have your company on this journey. Until our next leap forward, please be well.

Love,
Ray

REVIEWS

"Written in the past/present/future tense Ray Jane delivers words so nice that I had to read them twice.I'm sure the ancestors are proud as they are truly honored. Her poems tell us why she's mad as we share the feeling vicariously. Creating intention in a safely explosive atmosphere we share her love and rage. Entertaining and therapeutic Ray Jane delivers a soulful platter for your reading pleasure. It should be required reading in a world where books are banned."— **Baba Ngoma Hill (Go buy his book I Didn't Come Here to TapDance- A Poetic Memoir right now!)**

"The breadth and depth of Ray Jane's poems are intensely intimate yet universal in nature. Blending lyrical conventionality with unexpected deviations of prose this body of work is personal and political, deeply painful, yet full of joy. Probing deeply inward she exposes the emotions of Womanhood, Blackness, love, compassion, anger, heartache, grief and spirituality, Ray Jane rides the razor's edge. "Black Like That" demands attention, every line is full of rhythm and penetrating truths. This collection of poems touched my soul, challenged me, made me smile and brought me to tears. A must addition to your bookshelf, the taste of these poems will linger on your tongue.— **Jane SpokenWord, Poet & Spoken Word Artist, JaneSpokenword.com**

"*It was not supposed to/ hit/ like this/ I didn't expect my loving and logic/ to be stretched to the point where /it should have been painful/ instead, a rare joy came to visit me/ I should have stretched first/ cause my sense of luscious, delicious/ couldn't catch breath on this ride/ deep and reminiscent of every thought/ I was always so sure I had birthed myself / because it felt so true/ (sang like it was, anyway)/ Ought/ not/ to play wit folkses/ that/this way/ all bold no shame and abundance of in your game/ Had to drink Coca-Cola, Irish Breakfast, sparkling water/ to stay on the hydrated side/because the melanated side/ had been drowning in all the half dreams/ and lack of clarity/this world serves Black girls/along with bad promises and faulted mirrors/Til now/ Gimme another glass, please, Bartender/and set 'em up for my friends/ cause/ They/ We/ World/ are not/ready/for/this/and we be thirsty.*"— **Stacy Dyson, Poet - Acapella Vocalist - Playwright - TEDx Speaker - Author**

REVIEWS

"Who Is This Human?" Ray Jane invites us to view the world from her eyes, painting a portrait of how to make yourself big, when many do not want you to. She is known as "Thunder Lung," because she never shies away from authenticity. This collection will allow future generations to do the same. Ray reminds us "...that your body, still knows your language." — **Elizabeth Sophia Strauss, Author of** *Kundabeanie: A Book of Pankus, Inner Visions*, **Editor of the LGBTQ Literary Art Anthology** *Out Loud*

"The rhythms of *Black Like That* **are built for outrage as well as hip-shaking, both reverie and reflection. Ray Jane has crafted us a comprehensive ledger of Black personhood that screams our legitimacy in every single couplet. These are poems to get lost in."— Bendi Barrett, Author of** *Empire of the Feas*t

"This collection is a reminder of what it means to be "Black like that" Ray Jane's unapologetic truth rings through each chapter while paying homage to key players throughout past and present history. This is no ordinary book of poetry, it is a hymnal in an abandoned church singing praises to ancestors. Ray Jane creates relationships with words that redefines how you look at each line, and ultimately, the world. This is a journey or pilgrimage you must take into yourself both spiritually and emotionally. There are few writers/poets who can speak directly to you, but this collection feels like a late night conversation with a close friend. You will not be disappointed. Emotional, educated, and inspired maybe... but not disappointed." — **Shockie G The Poet, Author of** *In Lieu of Flowers*

"From its opening pages, beats and rhythms, The Drum thumps like an 808, echoing from these sheets of magic an intoxicating melody. With styles a plenty and grace unmatched, Black Like That: Poems from a Conduit draws readers in with magnetic energy. This Medicine Woman gives you a stunning view of the Black Woman Experience, from Black Thigh Thaumaturgy to For Sandra and Four Women Flying, Ray Jane keeps you engaged with stories of love and pain, with an affection for rhyme in sublime timing! Rooted in her faith, dedication and passion for poetry, and connection to her ancestors, this stands as living proof, this still exists and speaks loudly through her enchanted pen. Align your sights and put this book in your life! #ThundaLung #StormGodsInTheBuilding #Inhumans"— **Elemen2alPoet, Host, Author & CEO of Elemen2al Vis1onwrx, LLC. #StormGodsInTheBuilding**

"Ray Jane's Black Like That: Poems from a Conduit are a griot's signposts connecting a complex past straddled between bondage and rebellion, a present that demands society stand firm in justice and the future she desires to emerge from conjuring "pathways for the dead to rise." As each of her verses refuse "to apologize for her magic," Ray Jane fashion's portals out of poems for the reader to enter and exit time

REVIEWS

and space, but also the realization that Black and Brown bodies should "reclaim our time, reclaim our minds." Her poems demand Black liberation expand beyond "more than bondage and bandaged dream." Ray Jane's collection is a call to arms with Sankofa as a guide, the night's sky as a map returning breath to the body and an insistence that readers aim for "death defying feats, tightroping an infinity-glorious" and get free."— **Peggy Robles-Alvarado, Poet, Performer, Playwright, Producer and Founder of Robleswrites Productions Inc.**

"Ray Jane's long-awaited debut poetry collection predictably surpassed my expectations. From cover to cover, Black Like That pulls no punches. It is an eloquent, rhythmic, intentional and untamable battle cry. It's undoubtedly a landmark – the pages are are steeped in the pain, rage and pride that comes with being a Black woman. The book so artfully protests against the realities of racism and White Supremacy. It is the perfect blend of bold and gentle as it also serves as a love letter to herself, her family, ancestors and anyone seeking truth, a sense of belonging and healing. Every one of the pieces inspire us to speak our truths gracefully but unapologetically. Black Like That is an invaluable addition to our bookshelves – a must-have! "
— **Rosalynn Diaz, Author of *Lady Lotus*.**

Ray Jane's poems are old as drums, bones, and the medicine women who've used them. Her voice speaks for the unheard who haunt the human psyche. You give me Mahalia in your poems" — **Caridad "La Bruja" De La Luz, Emmy-Winning Poet/Actor/Indigenous Activist/Educator/Musical Theater/Bronx Living Legend/Executive Director of the Nuyorican Poets Café NYC**

Ray Jane is a Black female poet born in Brooklyn and raised in Far Rockaway, Queens. She uses her poetry to lift herself and other women of color. Always aiming to strengthen her voice, Ray Jane won the Verb Benders Slam Poetry team's inaugural poetry slam and is published, including pieces in Lalibreta.online an online poetry journal for Women in Creative Rebellion (2021, 2022), *Snarl: A Journal of Literature and Art* (2023), and *TESORO: 1st Anniversary Firesingers* (2023). She has participated in poetic writing workshops focused on empowering women like "RoblesWrites Presents: Respite, Write, and Release™ amongst many others and served as contributing editor for the anthology *Love Letters to Gaia* (2021). She has also moderated her own workshops with ¡Oyé Group! Poet's Corner (2021-23), and Art Defined Inc (2022, 2023). She currently serves as host of Freestyle Friday with The Word Is Write (2021-Pres) and previously hosted The Nuyorican Poets Café Thursday Night Online Open mic (2022-23). You can hear more of how she uses her voice in over 50 recorded poems on SoundCloud (https://soundcloud.com/jay-ray-11), walking around NYC on the app Hear, Before https://www.hearbefore.nyc/; and on several podcasts including We Be Imagining/Black Siren Radio, and Sound Minds Podcast's "Potent Women Wordsmiths". **For links** to all of this and more visit:

    ItsRayJane.com   IG:ItsRayJane   FB: Ray Jane

Printed in the USA
CPSIA information can be obtained
at www.ICGtesting.com
LVHW020349301023
762324LV00017B/924